# Ultimate FACTIVITY Collection

# SPACE

**DK** Penguin Random House

**Senior Editor** Wendy Horobin
**Senior Designer** Clare Shedden
**Designers** Stefan Georgiou, Charlotte Milner, Pamela Shiels
**Jacket Coordinator** Francesca Young
**Jacket Art Editor** Amy Keast
**Illustrators** Jake McDonald, Charlotte Milner
**Senior Pre-Production Producer** Tony Phipps
**Producer** Leila Green
**Creative Technical Support** Sonia Charbonnier
**Managing Editor** Penny Smith
**Managing Art Editors** Marianne Markham, Gemma Glover
**Publisher** Mary Ling
**Creative Director** Jane Bull

First published in Great Britain in 2016 by
Dorling Kindersley Limited
80 Strand, London WC2R 0RL
1 2 3 4 5 6 7 8 9 10
001–285430–Feb 16

A CIP catalogue record for this book is available from the British Library.

ISBN: 978-0-2412-3099-2
Printed and bound in China by L. Rex Printing Co. Ltd.
Discover more at **www.dk.com**

# What is space?

Far beyond our small world is an endless stretch of blackness that we call space. Although it seems empty, it is full of gas, dust, stars, galaxies, and planets like our own.

Don't forget to put your stickers in first.

Page _____

Page _____

Page _____

FIND
these pictures on pages 4–17 and write the page numbers in the boxes.

Page _____

Page _____

Page _____

**5** Up in the **exosphere** the air molecules can escape Earth's gravity and float off into space. Most satellites and space telescopes orbit here.

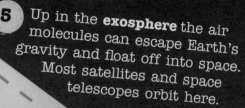

## FIND
each missing sticker and put it at the right level of the atmosphere.

**4** When you reach the **thermosphere** the air is very thin. The space station orbits in this layer, as will the first passenger space flights.

# Where does space begin?

Space starts at around 100km (60 miles) above Earth's surface, where the atmosphere (the gassy shell around Earth) begins to thin before disappearing entirely. There are five layers in the atmosphere.

Aurora

NASA counts anyone reaching this height as an astronaut

**3** Meteors burn up when they enter the **mesosphere**. The top of this layer is the coldest place on the planet.

The skydive record is 41,420m (135,890ft)

Weather balloon

**2** The **stratosphere** contains ozone, which protects us from the harmful rays of the Sun. Only special jet planes can fly this high.

Everest is the highest mountain at 8,848m (29,029ft).

Cirrus cloud

**1** The closest layer to Earth is the **troposphere**. It is where most of our weather happens and is the highest level at which ordinary aircraft can fly.

Cumulus cloud

Extends to around 10,000km (6,000 miles)

80–600 km (50–375 miles)

50–80km (30–50 miles)

16–50 km (10–30 miles)

16 km (10 miles)

If you could drive to space it would take about 1 hour at 80kph (50mph).

# What's night sky? in the

When it gets dark, you can look up and see tiny points of light. If you have powerful binoculars you can have a closer look at what's out there.

## Facts about...

### Seeing stars

Every star that you can see in the night sky is bigger and brighter than our own star, the Sun. You can see around 2,500 stars easily without using binoculars.

**1**

**Jupiter** is the biggest planet in our solar system. It has swirling bands of gas and lots of moons.

**2**

**Galaxies** are gigantic spirals of dust and gas that contain billions of stars. Our nearest neighbour is the Andromeda galaxy.

**3**

**Constellations** are stars that people have grouped into patterns that represent objects or animals. This is the Great Bear.

**4**

**Comets** are balls of ice and rock with long, dusty tails that streak across the sky on their journey around our Sun.

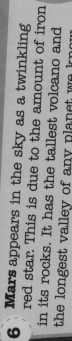

**6** **Mars** appears in the sky as a twinkling red star. This is due to the amount of iron in its rocks. It has the tallest volcano and the longest valley of any planet we know.

**5** **The Moon** is Earth's closest companion. Its surface is pitted with craters where it has been hit by meteors.

## Shining brightly

The brightest objects in the night sky are the Moon and the planets Mercury, Venus, Mars, Jupiter, and Saturn. A visiting comet may also put on a show if it has a spectacular tail.

# Our place in space

Earth may seem like a big place, but compared with the rest of outer space, it's incredibly tiny. This is how we fit into the scale of the Universe.

SPACE POST

Our star, the Sun, is one of billions in our home galaxy, the **Milky Way**. We are 30,000 light-years from the centre.

Earth is part of our **solar system**. It took the Voyager 2 probe 12 years to reach the solar system's furthest planet, Neptune.

The nearest world to **Earth** is our Moon. It takes three days to get there in a manned spacecraft.

## DRAW

a picture for your postcard from Al the alien. Don't forget to stick on a stamp!

**You are here** – or near somewhere like it. Even the largest cities are tiny specks when seen from space.

## Light-years away

Distances in space are so vast we measure them in light-years. This is how far light, the fastest thing in the Universe, travels in a year – nearly 9½ trillion km (6 trillion miles).

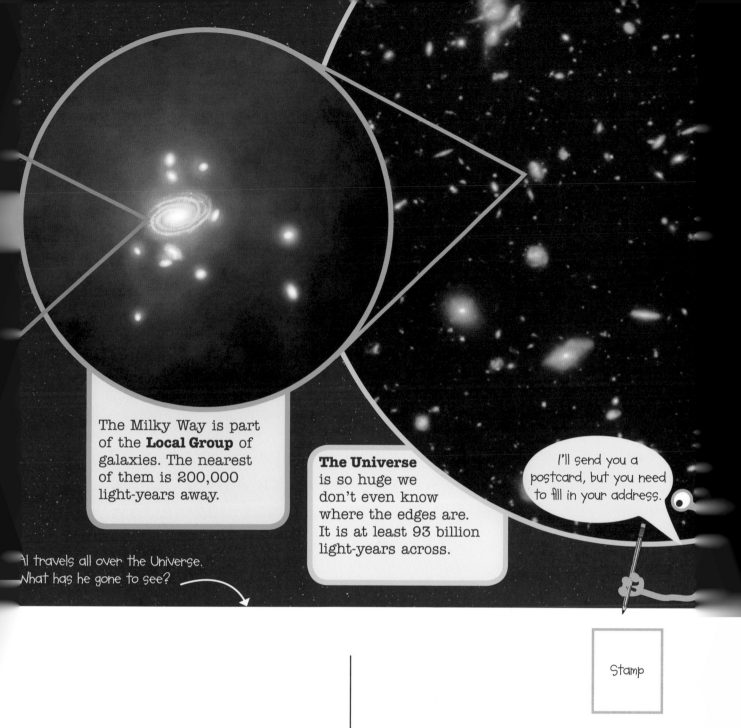

The Milky Way is part of the **Local Group** of galaxies. The nearest of them is 200,000 light-years away.

**The Universe** is so huge we don't even know where the edges are. It is at least 93 billion light-years across.

I'll send you a postcard, but you need to fill in your address.

Al travels all over the Universe. What has he gone to see?

Stamp

Name _____

City _____

Country _____

Planet _____

Star System _____

Galaxy _____

The Universe

Wish you were here!
Love, Al xx

# The SUN

**?**

**What is the Sun made of?**

**?**

**How hot is the Sun?**

Prominences are huge loops of gas that stretch hundreds of thousands of kilometres into space.

You can fit 110 Earths across the diameter of the Sun.

**How long does it take light to reach Earth?**

**?**

Solar flares are bursts of energy that show up as bright spots just above the surface.

Why should we never look straight at the Sun, even with sunglasses?

Because sunlight contains dangerous rays that could damage our eyes.

**FIND** the right sticker to answer these key questions about the Sun.

At the centre of our solar system is **the Sun**. The Sun is a star, which astronomers call Sol. It is not a big star compared to others in the galaxy, but you could still squash 1.3 million Earths inside it.

**How old is the Sun?**

**?**

**How far away is the Sun from Earth?**

**?**

Sunspots are cooler areas that appear as dark patches on the Sun's face.

*I'd better slap on some sun cream or I'll turn purple!*

**What is the solar wind?**

Probes keep track of the Sun's activity and warn us of any dangerous solar storms heading our way.

**?**

## Facts about...

### Future Sun

In about five billion years the Sun will **swell** and become a red giant star. It will then collapse to form a **white dwarf**, no bigger than Earth.

# The perfect planet

Earth is a very special place. Nowhere else in the solar system has exactly the right mix of ingredients that allow life to flourish. So what's the recipe for our perfect planet?

**Oxygen** There is plenty of oxygen in the atmosphere for humans and other living things to breathe.

**Water** Liquid water is vital to every form of life. It also regulates the climate.

**Friendly moon** Our Moon helps keep Earth rotating at a steady rate and pulls the oceans to create tides.

## STICK
the correct sticker in place for each ingredient, then draw an intelligent being.

All these things combine to make

## Facts about...

### Other Earths
Scientists searching for planets outside our solar system have found more than 4,000. Of these, **only about 800 are Earth-sized** and the right distance from their star.

### Home rock
Earth is a small, rocky planet with a hot, active core. Most of its surface is covered in water. Above is a thick, shielding atmosphere. Add in gravity to hold them all together and you have a rare type of planet.

**The Sun** We are just the right distance from our star: too close and we would burn, too far and we would freeze.

**Atmosphere** This acts as a protective blanket, keeping out harmful rays and space rocks, trapping heat, and creating weather.

**Hot core** Heat from the core keeps water liquid and brings new rocks to the surface through volcanoes.

**Plants** These filter out deadly carbon dioxide, make oxygen, and are a source of food for other living things.

Draw an intelligent being here. Who do you think that could be?

Earth just right for us to live here.

Nice planet, but those humans are funny-looking creatures!

**Intelligent life** Earth is packed with humans and animals that have learned how to survive in all sorts of tough conditions.

**TEST** your knowledge of the Moon and then colour in the phases on the page opposite.

The Moon doesn't shine by itself – it reflects light from the sun.

## I can see the Moon

**1** The Moon is **drifting away** from Earth by a distance of nearly 4 cm (1½ in) every year.

TRUE   FALSE

**2** The Moon was formed when another **small planet collided** with Earth billions of years ago.

TRUE   FALSE

**3** **Rocks** on Earth are older than those on the Moon.

TRUE   FALSE

**4** Scientists have discovered that the Moon has **moonquakes** that are similar to earthquakes here on Earth.

TRUE   FALSE

**5** The **dwarf planet Pluto** is smaller than the Moon.

TRUE   FALSE

**6** The Moon isn't spherical – it's slightly **lemon shaped**, with one of the pointed ends facing Earth.

TRUE   FALSE

From Earth, you can see at least 30,000 craters on the visible side of the Moon.

I wonder if it's really made of green cheese? I fancy a snack!

**If Earth (left) and the Moon (far right)** were the sizes shown here, this would be the

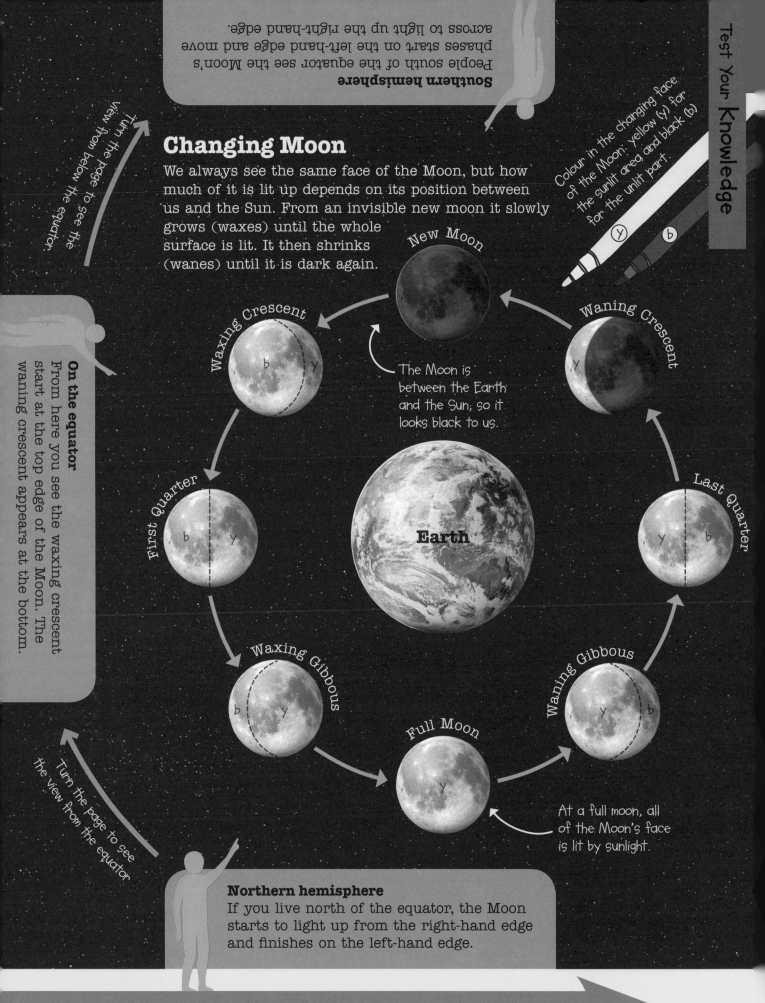

# Changing Moon

We always see the same face of the Moon, but how much of it is lit up depends on its position between us and the Sun. From an invisible new moon it slowly grows (waxes) until the whole surface is lit. It then shrinks (wanes) until it is dark again.

Colour in the changing face of the Moon: yellow (y) for the sunlit area and black (b) for the unlit part.

**Southern hemisphere**
People south of the equator see the Moon's phases start on the left-hand edge and move across to light up the right-hand edge.

New Moon

Waxing Crescent

Waning Crescent

The Moon is between the Earth and the Sun, so it looks black to us.

Last Quarter

First Quarter

**Earth**

Waxing Gibbous

Waning Gibbous

Full Moon

At a full moon, all of the Moon's face is lit by sunlight.

**On the equator**
From here you see the waxing crescent start at the top edge of the Moon. The waning crescent appears at the bottom.

Turn the page to see the view from the equator

Turn the page below to see the equator. View from below.

**Northern hemisphere**
If you live north of the equator, the Moon starts to light up from the right-hand edge and finishes on the left-hand edge.

distance between them. In reality it is around 385,000 km (240,000 miles).

# Eye on the SKY

## STICK
the stickers into the right places. Use the colours as a guide.

**Gamma rays** are given out by high energy objects, such as the black hole in the galaxy Centaurus A.

**Optical** telescopes such as Hubble can see galaxies like the Antennae better than those on Earth.

## Space telescopes
Putting a telescope into space lets astronomers measure types of light that can't get through Earth's atmosphere.

**Microwaves** and **infrared** are used to look for hot objects hidden by dust, such as this star nursery.

**Optical** telescopes collect visible light using mirrors and lenses. This cluster is called the Jewel Box.

All the objects we see in the sky are extremely far away. To get a better look we use tools called telescopes that collect different sorts of light and turn it into images that we would otherwise not be able to see.

## Ground telescopes
Land-based observatories use optical, radio, or microwave telescopes. They are usually built in remote, dry places high above the clouds.

The telescope Spitzer's **infrared** detectors pick up the heat from dying stars such as the Helix nebula.

**X-rays** reveal the hidden structure of the Cartwheel galaxy, as seen by the Chandra observatory.

**Ultraviolet** light is used by solar observatories like SOHO to watch the activity of the Sun.

**Radio** astronomy searches for energy sources, such as pulsars and galaxies that contain black holes.

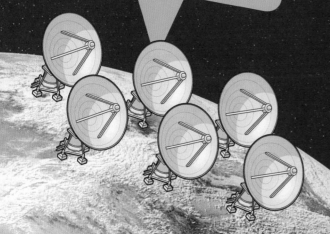

## Facts about...

### First light

Telescopes have enabled us to see some of the **oldest stars** and galaxies in the Universe. One star is 13.6 billion years old and is **still shining** – but only just.

# Probing space

Most of what we know about our solar system has come from sending out probes. Roughly the size of a school bus, these unmanned spacecraft are packed with equipment to analyse, photograph, and send data back to Earth. Some simply fly past their target, while others go into orbit or send smaller probes down to the surface.

**TRACE** the path of each probe to the right planet, then copy the picture of the crater.

**Lift-off from Earth**

1

2

3

4

5

Write the number of the correct probe in each box.

**Messenger** is the only probe to have orbited **Mercury** and mapped its surface.

**New Horizons** took the first ever close-up pictures of **Pluto** in July 2015.

**Voyager 2** flew past **Neptune** in 1989. It hasn't been visited since then.

**Saturn** is currently being investigated by **Cassini**, which is the fourth probe to go there.

**Jupiter** has been visited seven times. **Juno** will arrive in 2016.

## Ice spy...

This huge sheet of water ice was spotted in a Martian crater by the Mars Express probe. Its mission is to map the surface of Mars and analyse its rocks and atmosphere.

Copy the picture of the Mars Express flying over the crater and colour it in.

# The solar system

Earth is one of eight planets that go around our Sun. Circling along with them are moons, dwarf planets, asteroids, and the occasional visiting comet.

Page _____

Page _____

**FIND** these pictures on pages 20–33 and write the page numbers in the boxes.

Page _____

Page _____

Page _____

Page _____

Don't forget to put your stickers in first.

18

# Orbit quiz

The planets go around the Sun in a regular path called an orbit. It takes Earth a year to make one trip. Planets closer to the Sun take less time, while those farther out take much longer.

## READ
about each planet and write in how long you think it takes it to orbit the Sun.

225 days    12 years    165 years
84 years
29 ½ years    2 years    88 days

1 Giant **Jupiter** is the fifth planet from the Sun _____

2 **Venus** is Earth's hotter, faster twin planet _____

3 **Mercury** is the smallest and fastest-orbiting planet _____

The SUN

4 **Mars** takes twice as long to orbit as Earth _____

5 Our planet, **Earth**, goes around the Sun in _1 year_ _____

6 **Uranus** takes around a human lifetime to orbit _____

7 You would never have a birthday on **Neptune!** _____

8 On **Saturn**, days are short but years are long _____

## Near and far

There is an enormous difference between the inner and outer planets. Those closest to the Sun are small and rocky, while those further out are freezing-cold gas giants.

**The Sun** is the source of light and heat for all the planets in our solar system. The further you are away from it, the colder and darker it gets.

**Mercury** is the smallest planet. Its surface is covered in craters, making it look like our Moon.

Hello! This is where we live.

**Venus** is similar in size to Earth, but it is incredibly hot and is cloaked in thick yellow clouds that rain acid.

**Earth** is the largest of the four inner planets. It is the only place in the solar system where life is known to exist.

**Mars** is small and cold. It may once have had liquid water, but now it is a dry, rusty-red desert.

**Jupiter** is the largest planet. The stripes on its face are bands of clouds that swirl into giant storms like the Great Red Spot.

The **asteroid belt** is a wide band of rocky debris that lies between Mars and Jupiter.

## Facts about...

## The asteroid belt

Scientists believe that asteroids are fragments that were left over after the formation of the solar system. There are **billions of them**, but most are less than 1 km (0.6 miles) wide. They are usually named after people, but some have more unusual names such as Dizzy, Dodo, Brontosaurus, Wombat, and Humptydumpty.

# solar system

A group of planets that orbits around a central star is called a solar system. Planets form from the dust and gas left behind after the birth of a star. This is our family of planets.

**STICK** the planets in their proper place in the solar system.

**Saturn** is the second-largest planet, but it is so light it would float in water.

Saturn's rings are mainly ice and dust, probably from a smashed moon.

**Neptune** has five faint rings around its middle. The winds here are the fastest in the solar system.

**Uranus** spins on its side after being knocked over early in its life. Its rings and moons rotate up and over the planet.

Uranus's rings are made of dark dust and rocky material

# Postcards from Mars

Other than Earth, Mars is the most explored planet in the solar system. Four robotic rovers have crawled over its surface, and 42 probes have orbited around it. This is a tour of the must-see sights on Mars.

Hi, I'm Curiosity, the latest rover on Mars and your guide for this tour. Let's go and explore! First stop, Olympus Mons.

### Santa Maria crater
This stadium-sized crater was formed by a large meteor impact. It's young compared with some craters around here, but is old enough to have formed some sand dunes in the middle.

Stamp

### North Pole
The ice here is around 1,000 km (620 miles) across and 2 km (1.2 miles) thick. It's mostly water ice, but in winter it's so cold that carbon dioxide gas freezes and falls as snow.

### Valles Marineris
Five times deeper and ten times longer than the Grand Canyon, this valley system stretches a fifth of the way around Mars. It's a long way to the bottom!

Stamp

## MATCH
the stickers to the right postcard. Don't forget to put a stamp on it!

Stamp

**Olympus Mons**
This is the largest volcano in the solar system. It's three times the height of Mount Everest and almost as wide as France. Wow!

Stamp

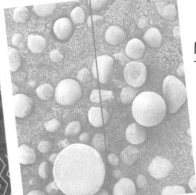

**Martian blueberries**
These pebbly spheres are full of iron. On Earth, mineral balls like these form in lakes, so they may be proof that there was once water on Mars.

Stamp

**Sand dunes**
Mars is as dry as a desert and covered in sand. The wind blows it into huge, crescent-shaped dunes. These are made of dark volcanic sand.

Wow – I never knew there was so much to see here!

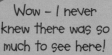

Stamp

**Dust devil tracks**
Sometimes the winds create mini-tornadoes called dust devils. These lift the lighter sand off the surface to show the darker sand beneath. Pretty, isn't it?

Stamp

**Sunset**
At the end of the day there's nothing better than watching the Sun going down. Sunsets are blue on Mars because of the way that red dust in the atmosphere scatters light. Time to shut down the batteries!

# Gas giant Jupiter

Jupiter is truly the king of the planets. This giant ball of gas has two-and-a-half times more mass than all the other planets put together.

**FIND** the stickers for Jupiter's moons and place them in the correct spot.

This is how big Earth is compared to Jupiter.

## Inside the giant

Jupiter doesn't have a solid surface. Its atmosphere is 5,000 km (3,100 miles) deep. Beneath it are layers of liquid and metallic hydrogen. However, there may just be a small rocky core at the centre.

Jupiter's stripes are bands of cloud that race around the planet in opposite directions.

White ovals are small storms in the cold upper atmosphere.

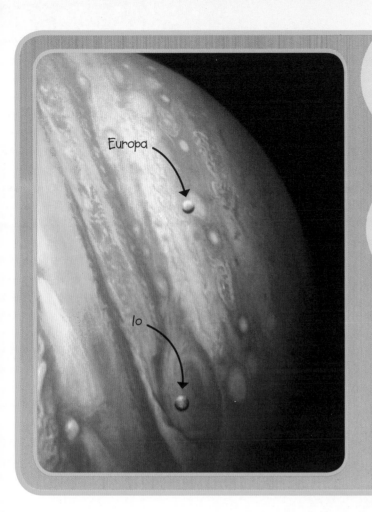

Europa

Io

## Many moons

Jupiter has 67 moons. The four largest are Ganymede, Callisto, Io, and Europa. The first three are bigger than our Moon and Ganymede is also bigger than the planet Mercury.

Ganymede

Callisto

Io

Europa

Find the moon stickers.

Galileo was the first spacecraft to orbit Jupiter and investigate its weather and moons.

Jupiter has a set of four faint dust rings around its middle.

### A great spot for storms

Storms on Jupiter can last for ages. The Great Red Spot is a storm that has raged for nearly 400 years. It is roughly the width of Earth, but is slowly shrinking.

## Facts about...

### In a spin

Jupiter rotates faster than any of the other planets. A day there only lasts **10 hours**. It spins so fast, the speed makes its equator bulge outwards.

I don't think my umbrella would last for long in that storm!

25

# Saturn's rings

Saturn is possibly the most beautiful of all the planets. It is surrounded by an icy ring system that is so large and bright that it shines when seen through a telescope.

## TEST

yourself to see how much you know about Saturn. Give yourself a star for a right answer!

## Ring king

Saturn's rings cover a distance of 280,000 km (175,000 miles) but are usually less than 1 km (0.6 miles) thick. There are three main and six minor rings, and a few incomplete arcs.

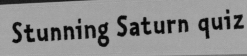

## Stunning Saturn quiz

### 1
**Saturn** is the only planet that would float in water – if you could find a bathtub big enough to put it in.

TRUE FALSE

### 2
The temperature at Saturn's **south pole** is much hotter than that at its equator.

TRUE FALSE

### 3
Its rings were **first seen in 1969** by the first man on the Moon, Neil Armstrong.

TRUE FALSE

### 4
Saturn is the **most distant planet** that can be seen without the aid of a telescope.

TRUE FALSE

I've been going around this ring road for days. Where's the exit?

Saturn's polar regions look blue in winter.

Its bands of cloud are not as clear as those on Jupiter but the weather is just as stormy.

## Facts about...

### Inner moons
Some of Saturn's moons orbit inside gaps in the rings. These **"shepherd moons"** keep the edges of the rings tidy by herding stray lumps of ice back inside.

### Icy halo
Unlike the dust rings of the other gas giants, Saturn's rings are made of ice. The pieces vary in size from tiny crystals to icebergs as big as a house. They are constantly clumping together and smashing apart.

**5**

It is **three times** further away from the Sun than Jupiter.

TRUE    FALSE

# Moons with a View

**FIND** and place all the sticker pieces that make up these scenic moon views.

Most planets in the solar system are orbited by moons. They are all solid bodies and some have an atmosphere. Made of rock and ice, they offer some of the most spectacular scenery in the solar system.

Our own **Moon** is a grey, airless world. Its outer crust was once molten lava but is now covered in craters made by meteors hitting the surface after it cooled.

**Titan** is Saturn's largest moon. Huge lakes of liquid methane lie near its poles. The atmosphere is thick and smoggy and its brown clouds rain methane.

## How many moons?

There are at least 173 moons orbiting the planets. Here we list how many moons each planet has.

| Mercury | Venus |
|---------|-------|
| **0**   | **0** |

**Ganymede** is the biggest moon in the solar system. A chain of craters across its surface show where the fragments of a comet pulled by Jupiter's gravity slammed into it.

On Uranus's moon **Miranda** is a long cliff that is six times higher than the Grand Canyon. A rock dropped from the top would take 10 minutes to hit the bottom because of the moon's low gravity.

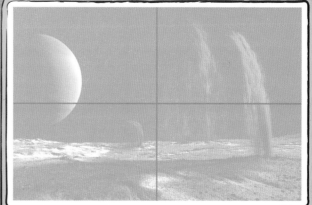

**Enceladus** is a tiny, icy moon of Saturn. Beneath its snowy crust is warm water that gets blasted upwards as jets made of icy crystals.

Volcanically active **Triton** is Neptune's largest moon. Its huge eruptions of nitrogen gas and dust can last a whole year.

| Earth | Mars | Jupiter | Saturn | Uranus | Neptune |
|---|---|---|---|---|---|
| **1** | **2** | **67** | **62** | **27** | **14** |

# Shooting stars

## What are they?

**Meteoroids** are lumps of space rock. Most are fragments left behind by comets and are the size of a grain of sand, but some are really huge.

When meteoroids enter Earth's atmosphere they become **meteors**. They are travelling so fast they start to burn up and glow with light.

A **meteorite** is a meteoroid that has survived its journey through the atmosphere and landed on Earth. Most meteorites fall into the sea.

**Asteroids** sometimes fall to Earth in huge fireballs. The results can be disastrous – one is thought to have caused the extinction of the dinosaurs.

If you look up on a clear night you may see a sudden streak of light flash across the sky. This is almost certainly a shooting star, or meteor, which is a fiery space rock.

**TEST** yourself to see how much you know about shooting stars, and find the stickers.

**2** Most meteors come from the surface of Mars or the Moon.

TRUE ○ FALSE ○

**1** Around 44 tonnes (48.5 tons) of meteorites land on Earth every day.

TRUE ○ FALSE ○

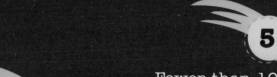

**Meteor showers** occur quite often throughout the year. The Leonids are a shower that appear in November. Hundreds of meteors an hour can be seen.

**5**

Fewer than 100 meteorites have ever been found.

TRUE ○ FALSE ○

**4**

Meteor showers only happen once a year.

TRUE ○ FALSE ○

**3**

Some meteors are bigger than a house.

TRUE ○ FALSE ○

**6**

The International Space Station is regularly mistaken for a meteor.

TRUE ○ FALSE ○

The Moon has lots of craters because it has no atmosphere to burn up meteoroids.

Oooh look – a shooting star!

## Facts about... Impact craters

Meteorites that hit land form bowl-shaped craters. Earth has been hit many times, but most craters have worn away. However some, like **Meteor Crater** in the USA, are still visible.

**31**

# On the surface

All the planets and moons in our solar system look very different. Some are bare rock, some have atmospheres, others are balls of gas, while many of the worlds farthest out are locked in ice.

**Jupiter:** this planet has a thick atmosphere of gases that churn and swirl at very fast speeds to create different coloured bands. Large spots shows areas where storms are raging.

**Io:** the face of this moon looks like a pizza because of volcanoes that are constantly erupting lava onto its surface. The lava contains a lot of sulphur, which gives Io its yellow, orange, and black colours.

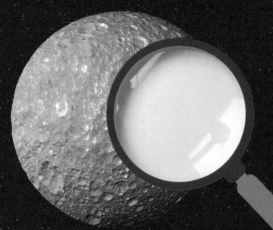

**Mimas:** this moon of Saturn is mainly ice with a small amount of rock. Its surface is covered in craters. The largest crater, Herschel, is the result of an impact that nearly shattered the moon completely.

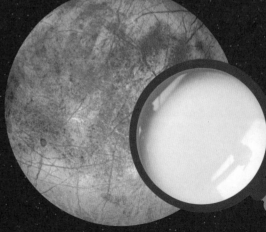

**Pluto:** this dwarf planet was shown to have a big heart when a probe flew past it in 2015. This icy ball of rock is reddish in colour and shows signs of mountains and craters.

Pluto's "heart"

**Europa:** Jupiter's fourth-largest moon has an icy surface that is crisscrossed with lines. These suggest that something under it is making the ice crack. Scientists believe that there may be a salty ocean moving beneath the surface.

## MATCH

the stickers to each of the planets and moons, then draw your own planet.

**Earth:** our planet is unique in the solar system because most of its surface is covered in water. This makes it look blue from space, with greenish brown areas of land, and wispy white clouds in the atmosphere.

Draw and colour in the surface of your own planet.

This looks like a cool planet to visit. What's its name?

# Outer space

Our Universe is almost too huge to imagine, and packed with billions of galaxies and trillions of stars and planets. It is so big, we can only see a small part of it.

**FIND** these pictures on pages 36–49 and write the page numbers in the boxes.

Page _____

Page _____

Page _____

Page _____

Page _____

Page _____

Don't forget to put your stickers in first.

# Universe facts

**TEST** yourself to see how much you know about the Universe. You won't believe it's true!

This picture is of an area of sky barely the size of a postage stamp. It looks empty when seen with the naked eye from Earth, but when the Hubble Telescope took a closer look, it was found to contain around 10,000 galaxies.

Hubble Space Telescope

Each of the blobs in this picture is a galaxy containing billions of stars.

**1** The Universe was formed in an explosion called the Big Bang around **13.7 billion years ago.**

TRUE  FALSE

**2** The Universe is **constantly expanding** – but it has no centre or edges.

TRUE  FALSE

**3** Astronomers estimate that around **275 stars are born or die** in the Universe every day.

TRUE  FALSE

**4** Everything in space is moving fast. You have **travelled 20,000 km** (12,000 miles) in the minute it took to read this sentence!

TRUE  FALSE

**5** There is a huge cloud of gas near the centre of the Milky Way **that smells of cabbage.**

TRUE  FALSE

35

## Galaxy shapes

Galaxies are collections of stars. There are three main types: spirals, ellipticals, and irregular. Most are dwarf galaxies, and many are believed to have a black hole at their centre.

**READ**

the description of each galaxy and write in which type you think it is.

We can see our own galaxy, the **Milky Way**, but we only see it as a band of stars and dust stretching across the night sky.

Hmm, which is which? Try reading all the clues first.

Irregular

Barred spiral

Dwarf

Spiral

Elliptical

Spiralling like cosmic fireworks, these galaxies trail long arms of gas, dust, and stars around a bright centre.

**1** _____ galaxy

Write in the galaxy name from the jumbled list.

These fuzzy, oval-shaped galaxies contain mostly old yellow and red stars with little or no gas or dust between them.

**2** _____ galaxy

# Gorgeous galaxies

So pretty! The Milky Way is a "barred spiral" galaxy.

The core of this galaxy is stretched out into a central bar of stars. Two long, trailing arms spiral out from each end of the bar.

**3** _____ galaxy

Full of gas, dust, and hot blue stars, these galaxies don't have a regular shape. They may be the result of two galaxies colliding.

**4** _____ galaxy

*It's much easier to see stars when you're far away from the bright lights of towns and cities, like at this observatory.*

Galaxies are among the most spectacular sights seen through a telescope. There are at least 170 billion of them in the Universe, each containing millions, billions, or even trillions of stars.

These smaller galaxies can be spiral, elliptical, or irregular in shape, but are only around one-hundredth the size of the Milky Way.

**5** _____ galaxy

37

## Main sequence star

**Typical star:** The Sun

**Temperature:**
5,000–6,000K

**Life story:** Average stars like our Sun are called main sequence stars. Depending on their size, they eventually turn into blue or red giants, or into dwarfs.

There are more stars in the Universe than we can imagine. But they're not all the same – there are different types that vary in size and temperature. Some are just about to blow up!

# Star struck

### Born in the clouds

Stars form in vast clouds of gas and dust. As they grow larger they eventually ignite, blasting jets of radiation through the cloud and sculpting it into unusual shapes that glow in space.

**STICK** the stars in place and learn about their star qualities and what makes them shine.

## Blue giant

**Typical star:** Alcyon in the Pleiades

**Temperature:**
20,000–50,000K

**Life story:** Blue giants are smaller and much hotter than red giants. They are very bright, but quickly run out of fuel and turn into a supernova.

## Facts about...

### Kelvin system

Astronomers use the **Kelvin** (K) system to measure star temperature. One of the reasons for this is that Zero degrees Kelvin is the coldest temperature in the Universe.

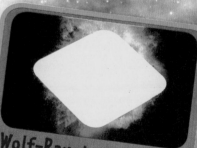

## Wolf-Rayet star

**Typical star:** WR124 in Sagittarius

**Temperature:**
25,000–50,000+K

**Life story:** These enormous stars are very hot and bright. They blast most of their outer layers of gas into space before exploding, then they collapse to form a black hole.

### Red giant

**Typical star:** Betelgeuse in Orion

**Temperature:** 3,000–4,000K

**Life story:** Once a main sequence star has used up all its hydrogen gas, it starts to burn helium. The star expands, but because its outer layer is cooler, it looks red.

### Binary or double star

**Typical star:** Main star, Pismis 24

**Temperature:** Varies depending on stars

**Life story:** Binaries are pairs of stars that orbit around one another. Doubles can look like binaries through a telescope, but the stars are actually far apart.

### Neutron star

**Typical star:** Crab pulsar in Taurus

**Temperature:** One million K

**Life story:** Neutron stars are tiny but are incredibly hot and heavy. Some rotate hundreds of times a second. Pulsars are neutron stars that emit radiation as they spin.

### White dwarf

**Typical star:** HD 62166 in Puppis

**Temperature:** 100,000K

**Life story:** When a red giant runs out of hydrogen it collapses in on itself to form a hot white dwarf. It slowly cools down to become a solid, cold, black dwarf.

### Supernova

**Typical star:** SN1987A in Dorado

**Temperature:** 100 billion K

**Life story:** A supernova is a giant star that has become unstable and has exploded. It is seen as a sudden burst of light as it flings its atoms into space.

### Red dwarf

**Typical star:** Proxima Centauri

**Temperature:** Less than 4,000K

**Life story:** These are the most common stars in the Universe. They are much smaller and cooler than our Sun, and very dim, but may burn for trillions of years.

# Stars in the sky

For centuries, people have been forming the stars in the sky into patterns called constellations. They are mostly animals, objects, or figures from mythology.

**FIND** the right sticker for each constellation then join the dots to reveal a picture.

**Leo** the Lion is easily recognizable from the sickle shape of its head and chest. It is one of a group of thirteen constellations called the zodiac.

**Cassiopeia** was a mythical queen. The five main stars form a sideways W. The central star in the W points to the northern Pole Star.

**Cygnus** the Swan contains the bright star Deneb in its tail. This area of the sky is full of nebulas and star clusters.

**Crux,** the Southern Cross, is the smallest of all the constellations. The bottom star of the long arm points towards the South Pole.

## Ancient shapes

There are 88 officially named constellations. More than half of them were first drawn thousands of years ago, and some even appear in cave paintings.

# Night hunter

One of the best-known constellations is Orion the Hunter. It is easy to spot because of the three close stars in his belt and the bright stars Betelgeuse and Rigel.

This is what Orion looks like in the sky.

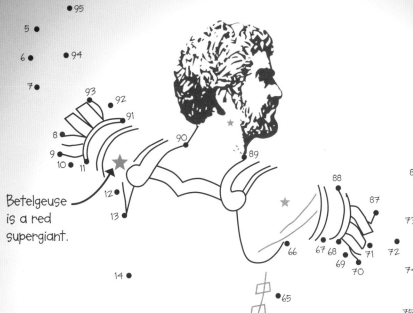

Betelgeuse is a red supergiant.

The Orion Nebula can be seen in the sword hanging from his belt.

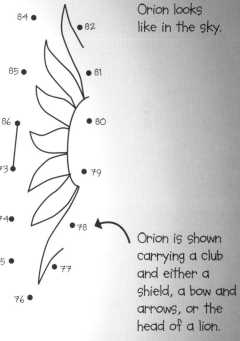

Orion is shown carrying a club and either a shield, a bow and arrows, or the head of a lion.

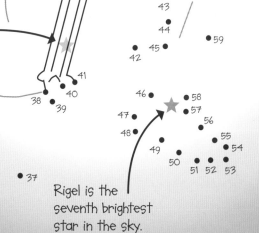

Rigel is the seventh brightest star in the sky.

## Facts about...

# On the move

Although stars may look close together, most are **far apart**. They are also moving, so the patterns we see today are slightly different from those seen by the ancients.

# A star is born

All over the Universe, stars are being born. The lifecycle of a star depends on its size, which also determines how it eventually dies.

New stars are forming inside the dust clouds.

**Hypergiants** are enormous but short-lived stars. They quickly become unstable, throwing off some gas instead of burning it.

Large protostar

When **protostars** get so hot they reach 10 million K (Kelvins) they ignite to become a star.

**Blue supergiants** are hot, massive stars. They burn hydrogen very quickly and last for a few million years.

**Average stars** like our Sun burn slowly and may last for billions of years.

Small protostars have less gas and make smaller stars.

## Star nursery

Most stars begin as a cold cloud of hydrogen gas and dust, called a **nebula**. If the cloud is big enough it starts to form swirling clumps that get tighter and hotter, creating **protostars**.

**READ** the text and find the sticker that matches the description.

Really large stars become **black holes.** We can't see them because their gravity is so strong that light can't escape from them.

The most unstable stars may simply explode in a **supernova** without going through another stage.

If the star has enough mass it may form a small **black hole.**

These stars expand into **red supergiants** and start to burn other elements.

When it has used up all its fuel, the star collapses, causing a huge explosion called a **supernova**.

Most blue supergiants end their days as a tiny, extremely dense, fast-spinning **neutron star**.

Watch out for the black hole!

When the star runs out of hydrogen it expands into a **red giant** and starts to burn helium.

Once its helium is gone, the star blows off its outer layers and becomes a **planetary nebula**.

What remains is a small, white-hot core. This **white dwarf** slowly cools until it loses all its heat.

# Voyage to a Black Hole

Your mission is to investigate a black hole and return safely to Earth. Don't get too close or you'll be pulled in and stretched out like spaghetti!

**7**

Make an emergency **spacewalk** to fix the engine. Go back one space.

**6**

**5**

Visit the **space station**. Move forward one space.

**26**

**25**

**4**

**24**

You spot a new **dwarf planet.** Move forward one space.

**36**

**35**

**3**

**23**

**Report findings** back to base. Move forward one space.

**34**

Hit a piece of **space junk**. Go back one space.

**2**

**22**

## TO PLAY

Roll a dice to move forward. Throw the exact number to land on Finish and win the game.

**1**

**21**

You hit a cloud of **interstellar gas**. Go back one space.

**Bad weather** delays launch. Miss a turn.

**20**

## START

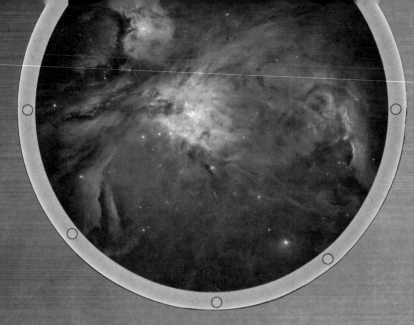

**Orion Nebula**
Hanging in Orion's sword is this huge nebula, which is creating new stars and solar systems, complete with baby planets.

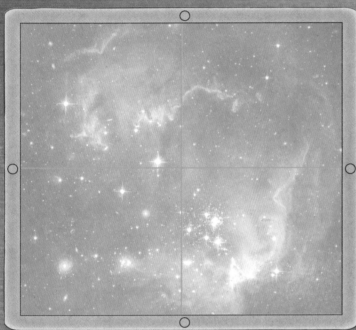

**Eskimo Nebula**
This nebula, made of bubbles of gas blown by a dying star and surrounded by streamers, was thought to look like a face inside a furry hood.

**Small Magellanic Cloud**
Hot, bright stars have formed in this area of our neighbouring galaxy. They are blasting out radiation that lights up the gas clouds.

# Amazing space!

**STICK** the stickers into the frames to complete these incredible pictures.

Space is full of huge clouds of dust and gas called nebulas. Some of them are places where new stars are born. Others are the remains of dying stars that are flinging their outer layers of gas deep into space.

### Carina Nebula
These long fingers of dust hide new stars. The horn-like spikes are jets of gas being fired out by the super-hot baby stars inside.

### Butterfly Nebula
This delicate butterfly's wings are actually jets of boiling gas being hurled out at supersonic speeds.

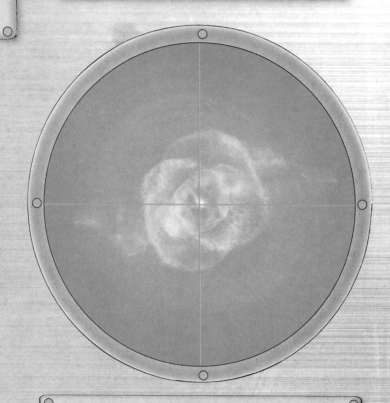

### Horsehead Nebula
Like a dark horse, this tiny part of the Orion Nebula rears out of the red clouds of gas around it.

### Cat's Eye Nebula
Staring out of the sky is a bright dying star surrounded by gassy shells that make it look like a huge cat's eye.

47

# Alien life

What makes you think an alien will look like me?

With so many planets orbiting other stars, there is bound to be life elsewhere in the Universe. These "aliens" could even look something like creatures that live on Earth.

Aliens in stories are usually based on humans and are presumed to be clever – but they might not be!

## Hot planets

Planets that are close to their star are likely to be hot and dry. Life there may be like our own desert animals – camels, scorpions, lizards, meerkats, and ostriches – that can survive without much water.

The thorny devil is a spiky Australian desert lizard.

## The pull of gravity

Gravity affects how life can grow and move. If gravity is high, animals are likely to move slowly and be close to the ground. With low gravity, life can move more easily and grow tall.

Colour in the two aliens on this page.

Slug–like animals may survive on high–gravity planets.

Opabinia is no alien – it once lived on Earth!

## Watery worlds

Creatures that live in water have to be able to swim or float. They may have big eyes or lights to see in the dark, fins, scaly skin, or a flabby body to cope with the pressure.

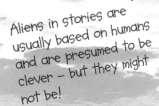

## Facts about...

### Space bears

Tardigrades, or water bears, are like little aliens, complete with their own spacesuit. They can **survive living in space** for up to 10 days without harm.

## Icy cold

Planets far from a star are cold and dark. Animals here may have thick coats; a good layer of fat; small feet, ears, and noses; and feelers to find their way.

Planet name:

**Tick** the boxes to choose what conditions your planet will have.

HOT

LOW GRAVITY

WATER

COLD

HIGH GRAVITY

LAND

**DRAW**

and colour an alien that could live on the type of planet you have chosen.

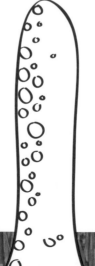

# Going into space

Humans have always wanted to explore space, but it isn't easy. Even getting off the ground is hard! You also have to take everything you need — air, food, water, and fuel.

Don't forget to put your stickers in first.

Page _____

Page _____

Page _____

Page _____

Page _____

Page _____

**FIND**

these pictures on pages 52–64 and write the page numbers in the boxes.

50

# Launch stages

**STICK** the rocket stages in the right order for a successful launch to the Moon.

5   The **Apollo spacecraft** travels on towards the Moon.

4   The **third stage** engine takes the rocket out of Earth orbit.

3   The **second stage** burns for 6 minutes, taking the rocket to a height of 185 km (115 miles) before it falls back to Earth.

An escape rocket pulls the command module to safety if there is a problem during launch.

Apollo command and service modules

# 5, 4, 3, 2, 1...

It takes an enormous amount of power and speed for a human to escape Earth's gravity and go into space. The **Saturn V** (left), which took men to the Moon, is the most powerful rocket ever to be launched. It weighed as much as 400 elephants when fully fuelled.

2   The **first stage** detaches when it has used up its fuel and the rocket is 68 km (32 miles) above the ground.

Third stage

Second stage

1   **Launch:** the main engines on the first stage fire, producing as much power as 543 jet fighters.

First stage

The noise at lift-off can be deadly if you're too close.

51

# Rockets

If you want to go to space, you need a rocket. Nothing else has the power or the speed to escape Earth's gravity. A trip on board one of these giant fireworks takes nerves of steel.

## Facts about...

### Rocket science

Rockets were first invented by the Chinese in the **12th century**. They were fitted with arrows, powered by burning gunpowder, and used as weapons.

**Ariane 5** This family of rockets is used to put heavy payloads into low Earth orbit.

**Delta II** A smaller rocket that has successfully launched more than 150 satellites.

**Long March 2F** China used this rocket to send its taikonauts (astronauts) into space.

**Soyuz** These Russian rockets are used to take astronauts and cargo to the International Space Station.

**Space shuttle** The shuttle couldn't launch itself, so it had to be strapped to three large rockets.

**Delta IV Heavy** Currently the only rocket capable of lifting heavy cargo into a Moon or Mars orbit.

**Falcon 9** A two-stage rocket that can carry satellites or deliver supplies to the space station.

**Saturn V** This three-stage rocket was used to launch the Apollo spacecraft on missions to the Moon.

**STICK** the rockets in place and draw one that will take you on a trip to outer space!

New rockets are being tested for future missions to Mars.

# The International
# Space Station

Bruce McCandless was the first astronaut to make an unattached spacewalk.

Astronauts have been living high above Earth for many years in the International Space Station (ISS). It is the biggest and most expensive spacecraft ever built, and covers an area the size of a football pitch.

**BUILD**
the space station using the stickers at the back of the book.

The main **robot arm** is used for lifting astronauts and equipment. There is a smaller arm on the Kibo laboratory.

There are **three laboratories** on the ISS. Up to 150 experiments are carried out, mainly on the effects of low gravity and on the health of the astronauts.

## Facts about...

### Trusses
A 109m (356 ft) **truss** system forms the backbone of the station. It supports the solar panels, carries electric cables, houses spare parts, and the track for the robotic arm.

Stick the Soyuz onto the ISS dock.

**Docking stations** enable rockets to bring new crews and supplies to the ISS every few months.

**Zvezda** was the first living quarters module to be installed. It can sleep two people and has a treadmill, kitchen, and toilet. It controls the ISS's life support systems.

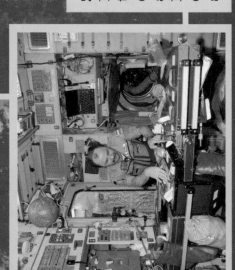

There are several **airlocks** that allow astronauts to make spacewalks outside the ISS.

# Living in Space

High above Earth, the International Space Station (ISS) is home to a crew of astronauts. They live and work in a space that is totally crammed with equipment and gadgets.

Strap yourself in for a good night's sleep!

Washing hair needs special no-rinse soap.

Grab rail

Daily exercise is vital to keep bones and muscles healthy.

## Daily routine

Every detail of an astronaut's day is planned years before they leave Earth. There are set times for eating, working, exercising, and maintaining the station. At the end of the day there is time to relax and call home.

Solar panels provide power.

## COLOUR

the inside of the space station. How many laptops can you count?

Objects float in space because there is no gravity, so astronauts have to tie everything down – including themselves!

You can spend your free time just hanging around.

There's always an experiment to do in the lab.

The views from the windows are spectacular.

It has taken nearly 200 spacewalks to build the space station.

Robotic arms are used for repairs and grabbing cargo ships.

Foostholds keep astronauts firmly anchored when working on the robotic arm.

## Facts about...

## Orbiting
The ISS goes around Earth at a zippy 27,700 kph (16,800 mph). This is so fast astronauts get to see 16 sunrises and sunsets every day.

# Day on the Moon

Only twelve people have ever set foot on the Moon. It is a difficult place to stay because it has no air to breathe and no water, but maybe one day we'll visit it again.

**COLOUR** the pictures to show what the astronauts did while they were on the Moon.

**1** After a journey of 385,000 km (240,000 miles), we fire the retro rockets on the lunar module and land on the Moon. We've left our pilot orbiting above us in the command module.

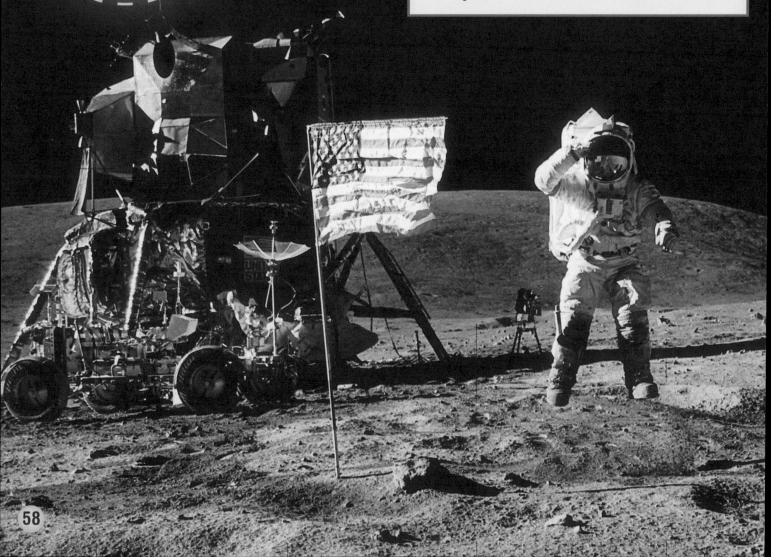

Draw in your own flag

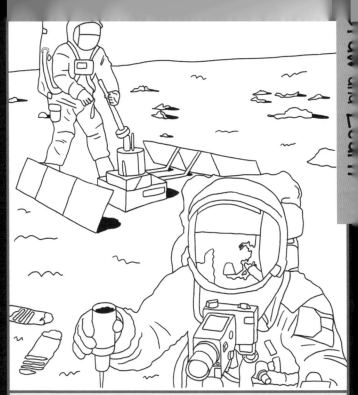

**2** We finally set foot on the surface. It's very dusty and grey, with lumps of rock and small craters everywhere. The first thing to do is plant a flag and take a few snapshots for the photo album.

**3** Plenty of work to do while we're here – collecting rock and soil samples, testing for moonquakes, and measuring the magnetic field. We film everything for the scientists back home.

Earth

**4** Time for a trip in the moon buggy to get some rocks from a nearby crater. If you put your foot down it can go at 13 km (8 miles) an hour! Hope that the batteries last the distance.

**5** At the end of the day we can relax. The gravity is so low here, you can jump higher than an Olympic athlete, even in a spacesuit. Luckily I packed my golf clubs. This ball should go for miles!

**Mercury 3**
This badge marks the first American astronaut in space.

**Apollo 11**
*Eagle* was the name of the first manned spacecraft to land on the Moon.

**Space shuttle**
The space shuttle made its first orbit of Earth in 1981.

**Satellite launch**
This shuttle mission put an Indian satellite into space.

# Mission badges

**STICK** the badges in the right spaces then design your own mission badge.

Every time there is a space mission, members of the crew design a new badge. The badge usually shows what the astronauts are going to do on the mission, such as launch a satellite or build a new part of the space station.

 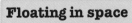  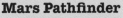

**Indian visitor**
India's first astronaut went to the Russian space station Salyut 7.

**Floating in space**
On this mission an astronaut did a spacewalk where they used a jetpack.

**Telescope launch**
Launching the Hubble telescope allowed us to see even further into space.

**Mars Pathfinder**
In 1997 a robotic rover was sent to Mars to explore the surface.

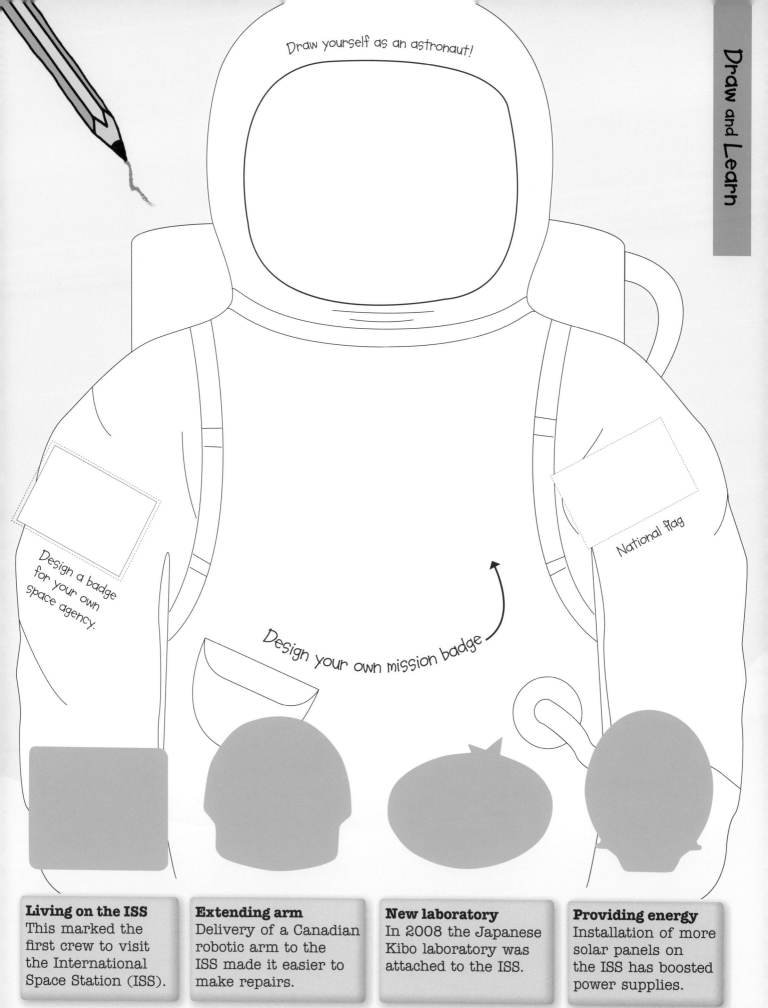

Draw yourself as an astronaut!

Design a badge for your own space agency.

National flag

Design your own mission badge

**Living on the ISS**
This marked the first crew to visit the International Space Station (ISS).

**Extending arm**
Delivery of a Canadian robotic arm to the ISS made it easier to make repairs.

**New laboratory**
In 2008 the Japanese Kibo laboratory was attached to the ISS.

**Providing energy**
Installation of more solar panels on the ISS has boosted power supplies.

# Life on Mars

**COLOUR** this scene of a colony of astronauts living on Mars with their pet dog!

It won't be easy to pack up and settle down on another planet. We would have to take everything we need – food, water, equipment, and lots of building materials – to survive for long periods.

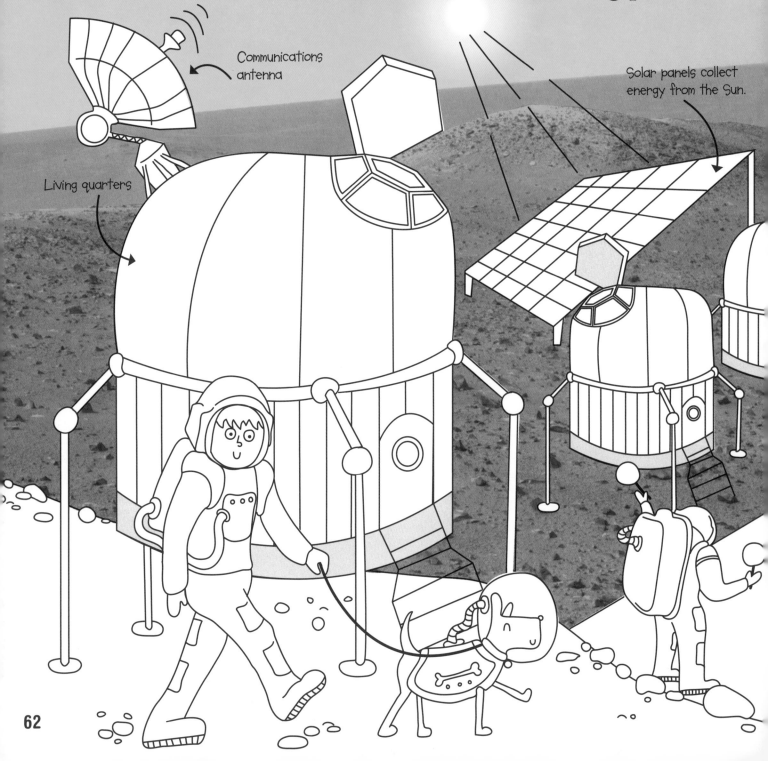

Communications antenna

Solar panels collect energy from the Sun.

Living quarters

# Destination Mars

There are plans to send people to Mars one day in the future, but with each journey taking up to ten months, it won't be a quick trip. Conditions on Mars are harsh – it's cold, has almost no oxygen in its atmosphere, and the water is frozen. Life as a Martian will be tricky!

## Facts about...

### Cavemen

The first Martian explorers could live in **caves** near the equator. This would protect them from deadly radiation and swirling dust storms that regularly sweep the surface.

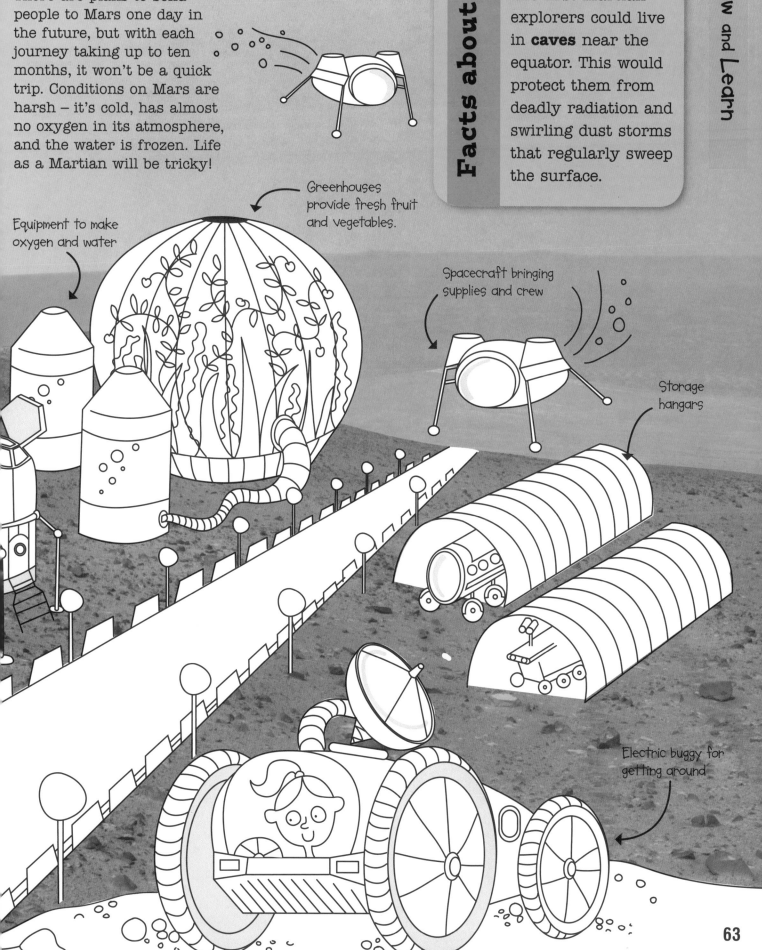

Equipment to make oxygen and water

Greenhouses provide fresh fruit and vegetables.

Spacecraft bringing supplies and crew

Storage hangars

Electric buggy for getting around

63

# Best-dressed astronaut

Space is not a nice place for humans. It's boiling hot in the sun and freezing cold in the shade. There's no air, but there is deadly radiation. To survive a spacewalk, you definitely need the right suit!

Life support system

**Helmet**
The helmet has two visors and contains communications and breathing equipment.

The undersuit contains liquid-filled tubes that help to keep the astronaut cool.

**Gloves**
These have special grips for holding tools and are heated to keep the fingers warm.

**Control panel**
This is fixed to the hard upper body section. It controls the life support systems and the communications equipment.

## Spacesuit facts

A spacesuit is a complicated piece of kit. It is made of 11 layers of fabric and is white to reflect sunlight. Suits are made up of different-sized pieces to match the build of the astronaut. It has to carry enough water and oxygen for the whole spacewalk.

Suits are made of separate parts that clamp together to make them airtight.

**STICK** this astronaut's spacesuit together to get him ready for a spacewalk.

**Boots**
The boots are soft and flexible so they can be slipped into footholds on the robot arm.

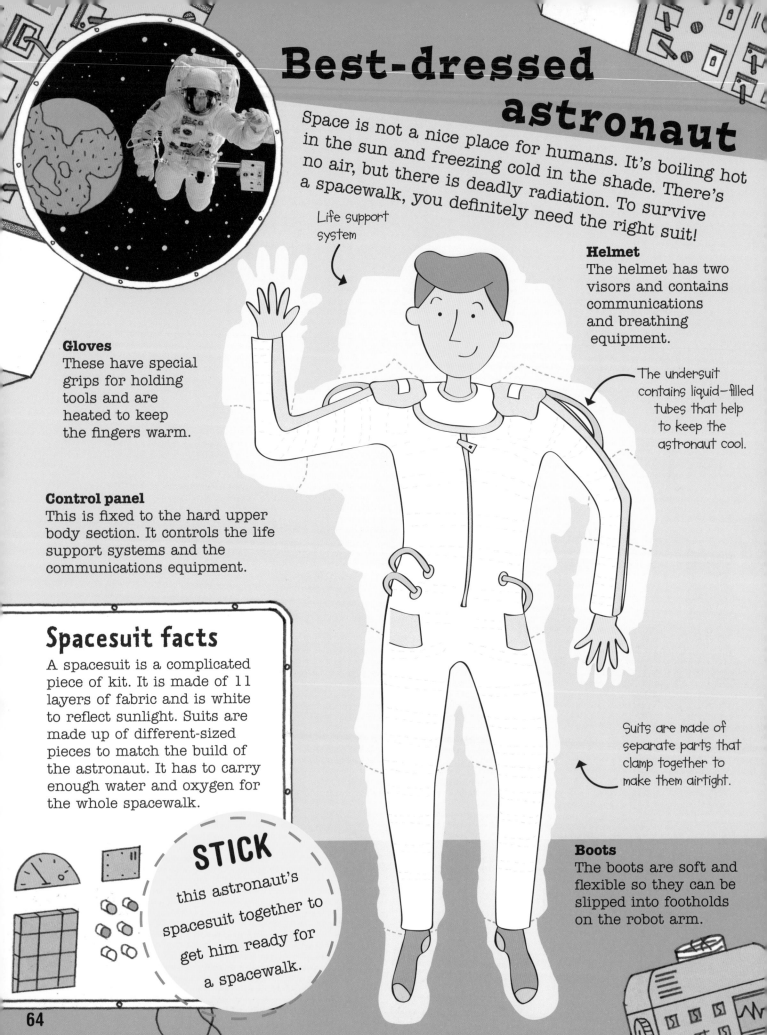

Use these to finish the diagram of Earth's atmosphere on **page 3**.

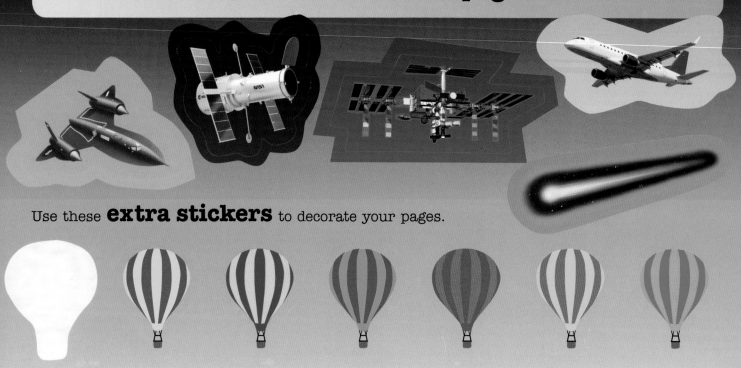

Use these **extra stickers** to decorate your pages.

These night sky stickers belong on **pages 4–5**.

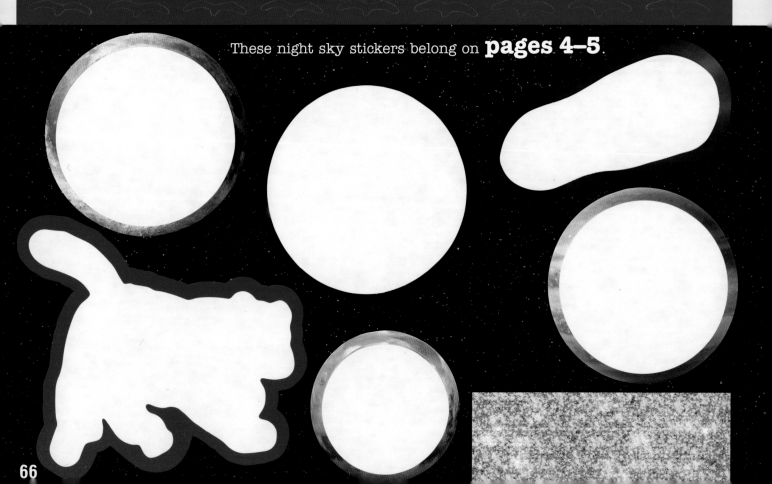

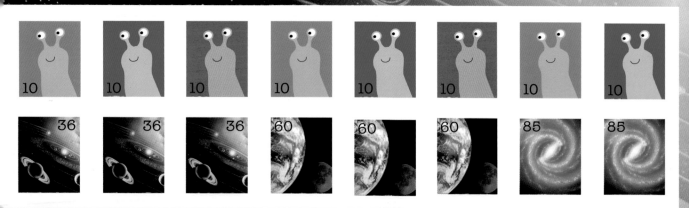

Choose the stamp for your alien postcard on **page 7**. There are plenty of spares, too.

Stickers

10 10 10 10 10 10 10 10

36 36 36 60 60 60 85 85

Use these **extra ones** anywhere you like!

SPACE POST SPACE POST SPACE POST SPACE POST

Stick these on **pages 8–9** to answer the questions about the Sun.

Storms on the Sun's surface blast **streams of particles** into space.

The surface of the Sun is **5,500°C** (9,900°F) but its core reaches more than 15 million °C (27 million °F).

It is made mainly of **two gases** – hydrogen and helium. It burns these gases and produces light and energy.

The Sun is **4.5 billion years** old. It is about halfway through its life.

It would take a jet aircraft 20 years flying nonstop to travel the **150 million km** (93 million miles) between the Sun and Earth.

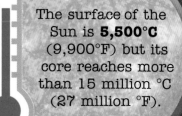

It takes light just more than **8 minutes** to travel to Earth from the surface of the Sun.

67

Stick the ingredients for the perfect planet on **pages 10–11**.

These Earth and Moon stickers are **extras** to use as decorations.

Stickers

These are **extra** probes and telescopes just for fun.

These views of Mars belong on **pages 22-23**.

These moons of Jupiter are for **page 25**.

The **stars** are for pages **26–27**. The planets are **extras**.

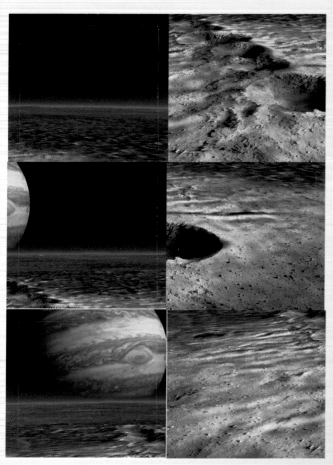

These shooting stars are for **page 30**.

These little planets and moons are **spares**.

These moons and planets are for **page 32**.

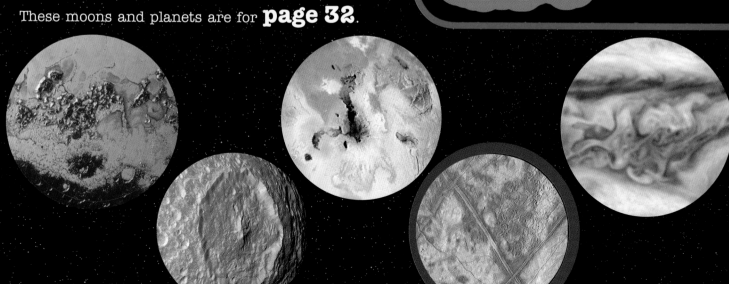

Use these **extra** star and galaxy stickers anywhere you like.

Place these pictures of stars in place on **pages 38–39**. Use the shapes as a guide.

These little stars are **extras**.

Put the constellations in place on **page 40**.

These stars belong on **pages 42–43**.

These stickers are for **decoration**.

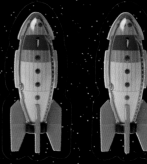

Use these stickers to fill in the nebula puzzles on **pages 46–47**.

These are **extra** constellations.

86

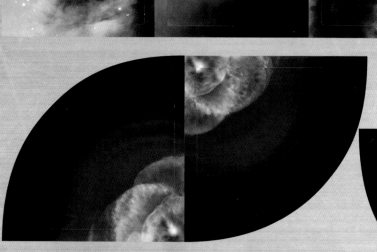

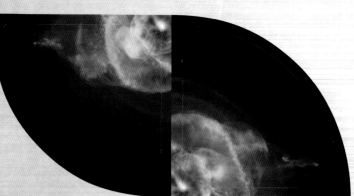

Use these aliens and stars as **decorations**.

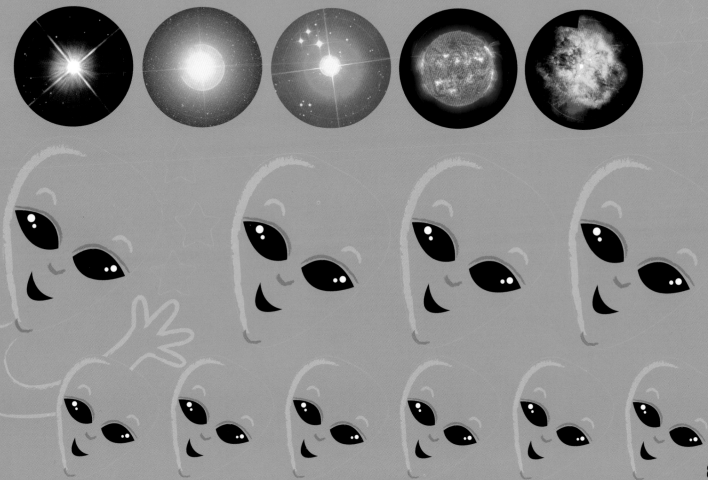

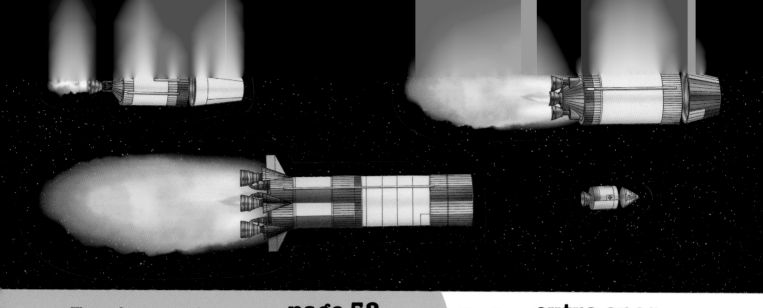

These famous rockets are for **page 52**.

Use these **extra ones** anywhere.

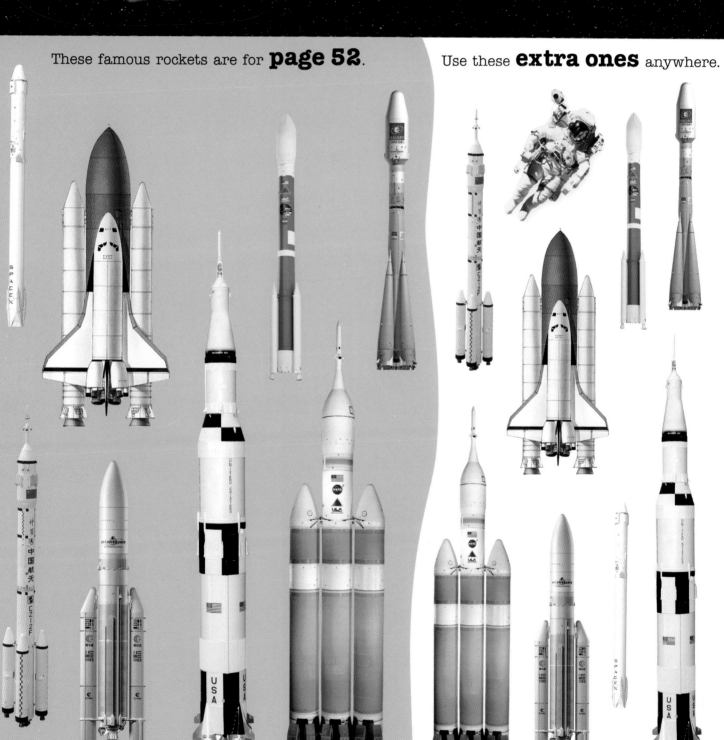

Build the ISS on **page 55** using these. The astronauts are extras.

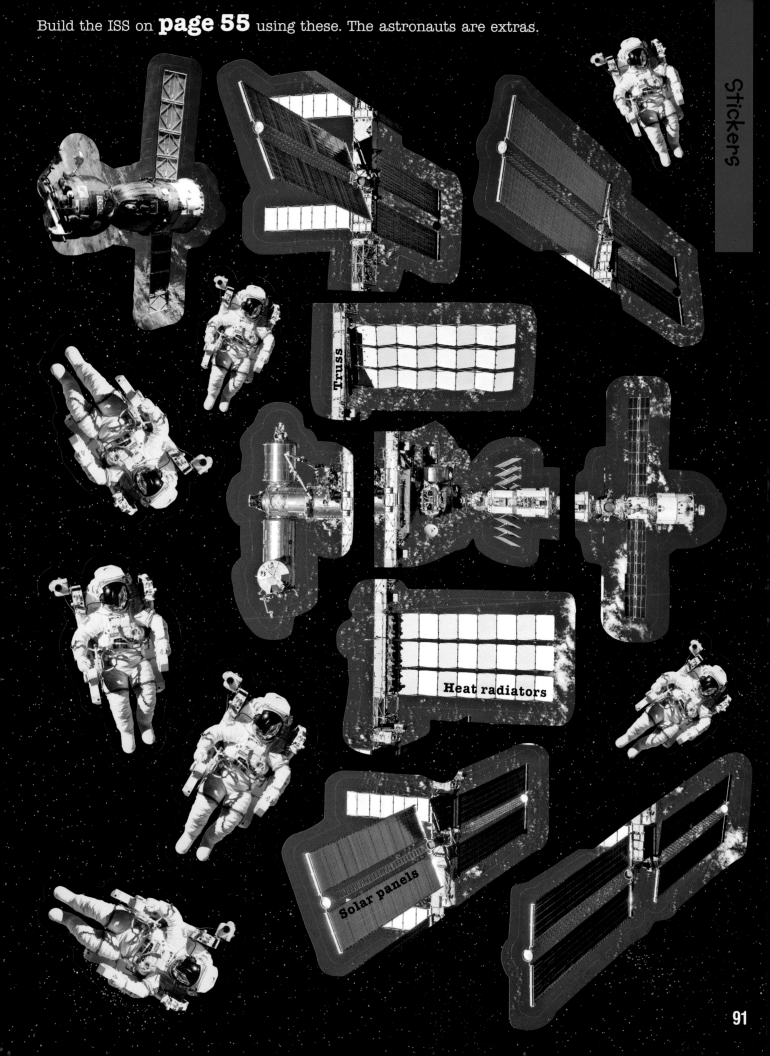

Truss

Heat radiators

Solar panels

Stick on the mission badges on **pages 60–61**.

Use these **extra ones** anywhere you like!